LEADING WITH CONFIDENCE

STUDY GUIDE

Leading With Confidence
Study Guide

How To Lead and Develop Others With Confidence

By

Miranda Burnette

Keys to Success Publishing, LLC

Atlanta, GA

Unless otherwise indicated, all Scripture quotations are taken from the *King James Version* (KJV) of the Bible.

Scripture quotations marked (AMPC) are taken from the *Amplified Bible Classic Edition.*

Scripture quotations marked (NIV) are taken from the *Holy Bible, New International Version.*

Scripture quotations marked (MSG) are taken from the *Message Bible.*

Scripture quotations marked (NKJV) are taken from the *New King James Version of the Bible.*

Scripture quotations marked (NLT) are taken from the *Holy Bible, New Living Translation.*

Scripture quotations marked (NASB) are taken from the *New American Standard Bible.*

Leading With Confidence: Study Guide – How to Lead and Develop Others With Confidence

ISBN: 978-0999893876

P. O. Box 314
Clarkdale, GA 30111

www.mirandaburnetteministries.org

Keys to Success Publishing
Atlanta, GA 30127

Cover and Graphic Design by Jackie Moore

TABLE OF CONTENTS

HOW TO USE THIS STUDY GUIDE

Whether you are leading a small group, teaching a class, or studying on your own, this study guide is designed for you to get a deeper understanding of God's Word, the Bible. In addition, this study guide will reinforce the principles taught in my book, *Leading With Confidence.* Here is how it works.

Step 1: Before you begin, please read the corresponding chapter in the book, *Leading With Confidence.*

Step 2: Read the *Lesson Summary,* the first section in this study guide.

Step 3: Answer the *Study Questions* in the study guide by referring to the material in the book, *Leading With Confidence,* the *Lesson Summary,* or the *Bible.*

Step 4: Once you have finished answering the questions in each lesson, turn to the *Answer Key* provided at the back of the study guide to check your answers.

Step 5: Answer the *Discussion Questions.* There are no right or wrong answers.

Step 6: Complete the *Life Application* Activity.

Step 7: Read and meditate on the list of *Scriptures* located at the end of each lesson. If you desire, you may also memorize some of the scripture verses. This is an important step because those scripture verses are the basis of the teaching in each lesson.

Step 8: Read the list of *Inspirational Quotes* located at the end of each lesson.

Materials Needed: Bible, Study Guide, the book, *Leading With Confidence,* and a writing utensil.

INTRODUCTION

Confidence is about believing in yourself, feeling good about yourself, and feeling confident about your abilities. Being a confident leader is about having a "Can-Do" attitude and believing that you can reach your goals and achieve great things.

This book is about being yourself, having confidence to be who you are, and leading others confidently. It is about being the unique individual God created you to be. If you are a leader, never try to hide your uniqueness. Instead, be thankful for it. Don't be afraid to be you. Be yourself. Who else is better qualified?

Always be a first-rate version of yourself, instead of a second-rate version of somebody else.

—Judy Garland

A leader with confidence will accomplish more than a leader without confidence. When we find out who we are in the Lord and become secure in that knowledge, we don't have to try to be somebody we are not, and we don't have to go around comparing ourselves to others.

Instead of focusing on what others have, focus on what makes you who you are. We don't have to put others down to make ourselves look good. Until you learn to accept who you are and work to address your flaws, you will never grow as a leader.

Ralph Waldo Emerson said, "The creation of a thousand forests is in one acorn."

It doesn't matter where you are right now in life; you can grow to be someone great. In addition, you can also help many other people grow to reach their full potential.

Galatians 5:1 (KJV) says, "Stand fast therefore in the liberty wherewith Christ hath made us free, and be not entangled again with the yoke of bondage.

Walk in your freedom in Christ. We are free to be ourselves in Christ. Relax and be yourself. Be happy with who you are. God made you an original, not a copy.

Ethel Waters said, "I know I'm somebody, 'cause God don't make no junk."

Don't try to be like someone else. Each individual has different strengths and weaknesses. The word *individual* means separate, distinguished by specific attributes or identifying traits, distinct or unique. Don't try to be someone you are not. If you be yourself, in spite of your flaws, we all have them, people will respect you more. It takes courage to be yourself. Be a courageous leader.

Be the best you, you can be. You are one of a kind. You are valuable to God.

Luke 12:7 (ESV) says, "Why, even the hairs of your head are all numbered. Fear not; you are of more value than many sparrows."

God is for you, and he wants you to be for you too. A quote by an unknown author says this:

"If you really put a small value upon yourself, rest assured that the world will not raise your price."

__Author Unknown

Are you for yourself or against yourself? Zig Ziglar said this:

"You can't consistently perform in a manner inconsistent with the way you see yourself."

__Zig Ziglar

Know who you are in Christ. True leadership involves who you are or who you are becoming, as opposed to what you do. Who you are consists of how you think and what you value.

Proverbs 23:7 (NKJV) says, "For as he thinks in his heart, so is he…"

To be a great leader, you have to believe you are a great leader. God always focuses on our inward qualities or our heart. God is concerned about our character, which is who we are. Our character has more to do with who we are on the inside rather than who we present ourselves to be on the outside. Our character is who we are when no one is looking.

Our character and inward qualities take time to develop in our lives. However, as they develop, our confidence as a leader increases, and our attitude becomes more positive because our attitude and confidence as a leader are related.

To be an effective leader, starts with integrity of the heart. Integrity is more important than ability. You can train a person to do the job, but if the person doesn't have integrity, you have a problem on your hands.

Integrity means firm adherence to a code of especially moral or artistic values, an unimpaired condition, the quality or state of being complete or undivided *(Merriam Webster)*. Integrity also means being the same inside and outside. It means your actions match your words, and you will do what you said you would do.

Philippians 4:13 (AMPC) says, "I have strength for all things in Christ Who empowers me [I am ready for anything and equal to anything through Him Who infuses inner strength into me; I am self-sufficient in Christ's sufficiency].

We are self-sufficient in Christ's sufficiency. Whatever we do, we do it through Christ.

Philippians 4:13 (NKJV) says, "I can do all things through Christ who strengthens me."

Your confidence must come from God. You are not sufficient by yourself. Remember, don't try to be like someone else. Be the leader God has called you to be. Lead the way God leads you to do it. Put your trust in God and lean and depend on Him. Don't try to do it in your own ability, but in God's ability and strength.

You CAN do all things, even lead with confidence, through Christ. Therefore, to be that dynamic leader you would like to be, start LEADING WITH CONFIDENCE today!

LESSON 1

CHARACTERISTICS OF A CONFIDENT LEADER

LESSON SUMMARY

What is your idea of a confident and effective leader? Is it someone who has the ability to remain calm under pressure, give people clear directives, and inspire others? Does leadership involve being forceful and direct? Everyone comes to the table with their own idea of what a leader is, and often that perception is shaped by past experiences, beliefs, and the influence of someone who was once in a position of leadership over them.

Confidence is an essential characteristic of leaders. The word confidence, according to *Webster,* means trust or faith, a feeling of assurance, especially self-assurance or security. Confidence in the *Greek* implies a quality of assurance that leads one to undertake a thing. It means a belief that you are able and acceptable. Confidence causes one to be bold, open, or plain.

Confidence is vital to our leadership success. It is crucial if you are going to accomplish anything in life. That is why the writer of Hebrews urges us in the following verse not to throw away our confidence. *Hebrews 10:35 (NIV) says, "So do not throw away your confidence; it will be richly rewarded."* Don't throw your confidence away!

Leadership is more than a title or position. True leadership is marked by influence, faithfulness, and ability. Influence is probably the most important characteristic of a true leader. As a confident leader, your faithfulness will be tested regularly.

STUDY QUESTIONS

1. A confident leader is someone who has the ability to do what?

   _____

   _____

   _____

2. Name two things leadership does not involve.

   _____

   _____

   _____

3. What is *Webster's* definition of confidence?

   _____

   _____

   _____

4. Read *Hebrews 10:35 (NIV).* What does the writer urge us not to throw away? Why?

   _____

   _____

   _____

5. Name three characteristics of a confident leader.

   _____

   _____

   _____

DISCUSSION QUESTIONS

1. Why do you think confidence is so vital to a leader's success?

_____

_____

_____

2. Explain why leadership is more than a title or position.

_____

_____

_____

_____

3. What does the word *faithfulness* mean?

_____

_____

_____

4. How is confidence contagious?

_____

_____

_____

5. How can a leader actively demonstrate faithfulness?

_____

_____

_____

_____

LIFE APPLICATION

As a leader, what are several ways you can empower or equip those whom you lead to be strong, confident leaders? Reflect and write about this on the following page.

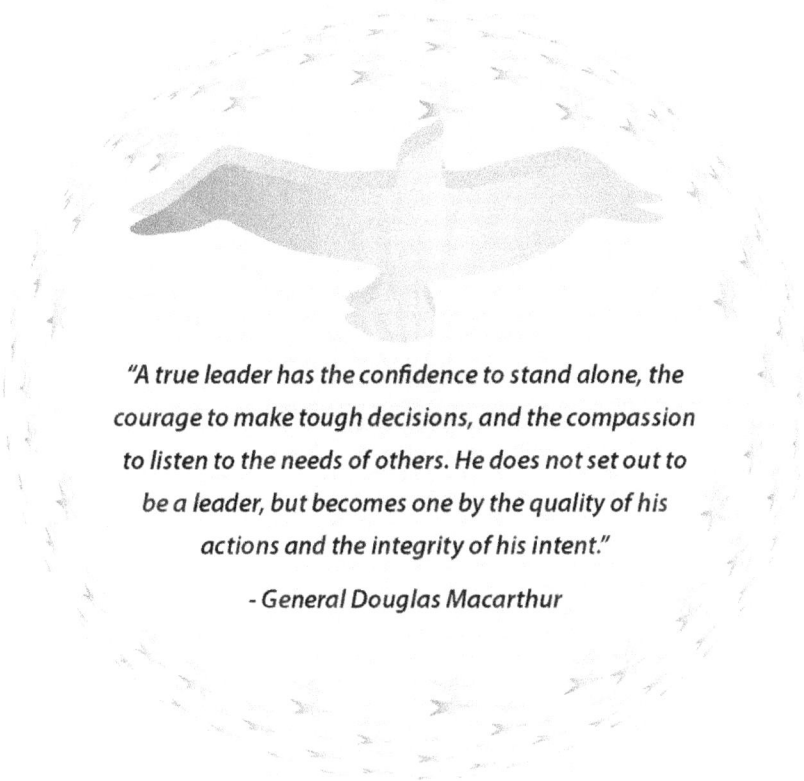

"A true leader has the confidence to stand alone, the courage to make tough decisions, and the compassion to listen to the needs of others. He does not set out to be a leader, but becomes one by the quality of his actions and the integrity of his intent."

- General Douglas Macarthur

Empowering Others To Lead

Write & Reflect

_____

_____

_____

_____

_____

_____

_____

_____

_____

_____

_____

_____

_____

_____

SCRIPTURES

Stand fast therefore in the liberty wherewith Christ hath made us free, and be not entangled again with the yoke of bondage.

Galatians 5:1 (KJV)

Why, even the hairs of your head are all numbered. Fear not; you are of more value than many sparrows.

Luke 12:7 (ESV)

I have strength for all things in Christ Who empowers me [I am ready for anything and equal to anything through Him Who infuses inner strength into me; I am self-sufficient in Christ's sufficiency].

Philippians 4:13 (AMPC)

I can do all things through Christ who strengthens me.

Philippians 4:13 (NKJV)

So do not throw away your confidence; it will be richly rewarded.

Hebrews 10:35 (NIV)

For as he thinks in his heart, so is he...

Proverbs 23:7 (NKJV)

INSPIRATIONAL QUOTES

"Always be a first-rate version of yourself, instead of a second-rate version of somebody else."

__Judy Garland

"The creation of a thousand forests is in one acorn."

Ralph Waldo Emerson

I know I'm somebody, 'cause God don't make no junk."

Ethel Waters

"If you really put a small value upon yourself, rest assured that the world will not raise your price."

__Author Unknown

"You can't consistently perform in a manner inconsistent with the way you see yourself."

__Zig Ziglar

"A true leader has the confidence to stand alone, the courage to make tough decisions, and the compassion to listen to the needs of others. He does not set out to be a leader, but becomes one by the quality of his actions and the integrity of his intent."

__General Douglas Macarthur

LESSON 2

A CONFIDENT LEADER GETS RESULTS

LESSON SUMMARY

Effective leaders produce results. The measure of success is demonstrated when you, the leader, is not present. How smoothly your organization runs when you are not around is a reflection of your true leadership ability. It shows how well you have trained and imparted your vision and objectives into the hearts of your team.

One major hindrance to having a successful organization is being a leader who has what is called *The Octopus Mentality.* This is when you feel you must have your hands in everything. When you do this, you hinder the growth and leadership potential of others who could do the job and make things easier for you. When you train others to do their jobs in excellence and give them the liberty to make mistakes, you demonstrate your own leadership skills.

One of the main reasons failure occurs in leadership is a lack of proper orientation and training. To *orient* means to make someone familiar with something or to acquaint with the existing situation or environment *(Webster).* Once you initially orient someone with the basics, then and only then does the training begin.

Part of operating as a confident leader is also having confidence in yourself and your selective decisions. It is up to you, the leader, to make sure knowledge is effectively imparted and executed to boost the confidence of your followers.

STUDY QUESTIONS

1. How is a leader's true leadership ability shown or reflected in his or her organization?

_____

_____

2. What is one of the main reasons failure occurs in leadership?

_____

_____

3. What does it mean to *orient*?

_____

_____

4. Once you initially orient someone with the basics, what comes next?

_____

_____

5. Part of operating as a confident leader is also having confidence in _____ and your selective _____.

DISCUSSION QUESTION

1. Explain what it means for a leader to have an *"Octopus Mentality."*

_____

_____

_____

2. Why do you think it is so important for a leader to have relational skills?

_____

_____

3. What are a few simple ways for a leader to build strong connections with his or her staff or team?

_____

_____

4. How can a leader communicate more confidence to his or her followers and their abilities?

_____

_____

_____

5. What are *"The Big Three"* that will set you on the course to successful, confident leadership?

_____

_____

_____

_____

LIFE APPLICATION

How can you, the leader, create an atmosphere of care in your company or organization? Reflect and write about ways you can do this on the following page.

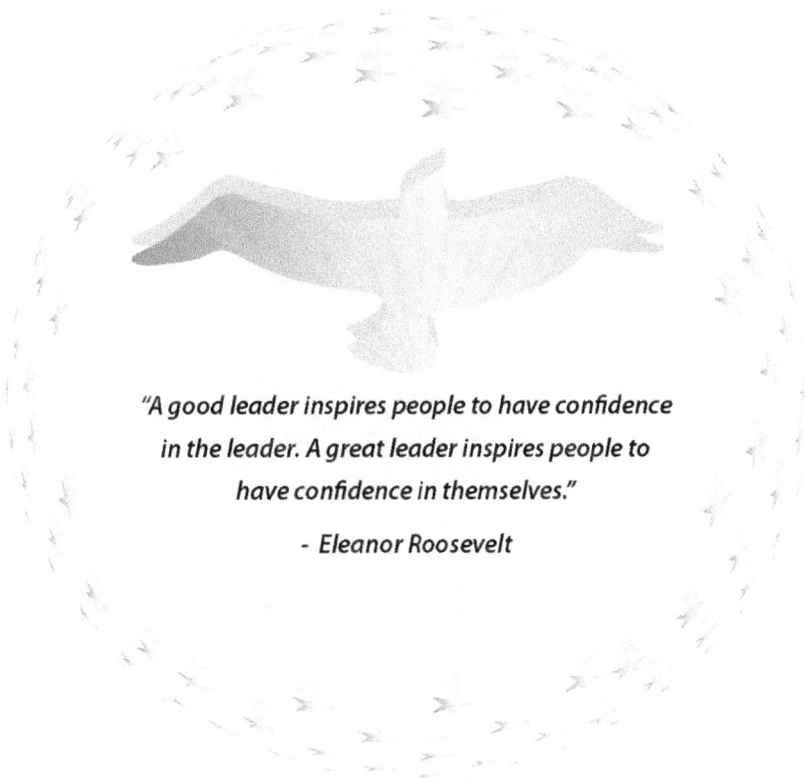

"A good leader inspires people to have confidence in the leader. A great leader inspires people to have confidence in themselves."

- Eleanor Roosevelt

Creating an Atmosphere of Caring

Write & Reflect

_____

_____

_____

_____

_____

_____

_____

_____

_____

_____

_____

_____

_____

_____

SCRIPTURES

In the fear of the Lord there is strong confidence, And his children will have refuge.

Proverbs 14:26 (NASB)

For the Lord will be your confidence And will keep your foot from being caught.

Proverbs 3:26 (NASB)

INSPIRATIONAL QUOTES

"Nobody cares how much you know, until they know how much you care."

__Theodore Roosevelt

"A good leader inspires people to have confidence in the leader. A great leader inspires people to have confidence in themselves."

__Eleanor Roosevelt

LESSON 3

CONFIDENT LEADERS REPRODUCE CONFIDENT LEADERS

LESSON SUMMARY

Confident leaders must model the desired behavior to those who follow them. As a confident leader, you must demonstrate the qualities you want to see in others. Confident leaders carry themselves a certain way. Therefore, they are effective in leading by example.

Leading by example is not just done where exterior appearances are concerned, but more importantly, with character and integrity. Your decision to live the principles of God's Word creates a standard others will want to follow. The Bible gives clear guidelines, which dictate how confident leaders should conduct themselves. By aligning your life with these standards, you position yourself to have people follow you who operate the same way.

If you want others to follow you, you must strive to be a good example! You must be a leader who is confident, grounded, and effective in allowing others to follow you. This requires walking in the love of God and according to His Word.

As a confident leader, one of the keys to your success is maintaining contact with your Heavenly Father daily. Surprisingly, many may wonder how to maintain daily contact with God. The answer is simple; through Bible study, regular prayer, and praising God. These are vital components to keeping your relationship with the Father fresh and flourishing and will help you, as a leader, know God's will and to fulfill it.

STUDY QUESTIONS

1. If a leader wants to see good qualities in those who follow him, what must he do?

   _____

   _____

2. Leading by example is not just done where exterior appearances are concerned, but more importantly with what?

   _____

   _____

3. What does your decision to live the principles of God's Word create?

   _____

   _____

4. Read *Proverbs 16:12 (MSG).* What does this verse tell us about good leaders and sound leadership?

   _____

   _____

   _____

   _____

5. As a confident leader, what is one of the keys to your success?

   _____

   _____

DISCUSSION QUESTIONS

1. What are some examples of how a confident leader can model the desired behavior to those who follow him or her?

   _____

   _____

   _____

2. Read *Proverbs 29:12 (MSG)*. As a leader, what does this verse mean to you?

   _____

   _____

   _____

3. According to *2 Timothy 2:24 (AMP)*, what must the servant of the Lord not participate in?

   _____

   _____

4. According to *2 Timothy 2:24 (AMP)*, what must the servant of the Lord be?

   _____

   _____

5. How can a leader maintain daily contact with God?

   _____

   _____

   _____

LIFE APPLICATION

On the following page, write down five ways, you as a leader can lead by example.

"At its core, I believe leadership is about instilling confidence in others."

- Howard Schultz

Lead By Example

Write & Reflect

_____

_____

_____

_____

_____

_____

_____

_____

_____

_____

_____

_____

_____

SCRIPTURES

The servant of the Lord must not participate in quarrels, but must be kind to everyone [even-tempered, preserving peace, and he must be], skilled in teaching, patient and tolerant when wronged.

2 Timothy 2:24 (AMP)

Good leaders abhor wrongdoing of all kinds; sound leadership has a moral foundation.

Proverbs 16:12 (MSG)

When a leader listens to malicious gossip, all the workers get infected with evil.

Proverbs 29:12 (MSG)

Good-tempered leaders invigorate lives; they're like spring rain and sunshine.

Proverbs 16:15 (MSG)

INSPIRATIONAL QUOTES

"At its core, I believe leadership is about instilling confidence in others."

_Howard Schultz

LESSON 4

GOD'S WORD + PRAYER = CONFIDENCE

LESSON SUMMARY

The Word of God is the spiritual food you need to keep you operating in *confidence overflow.* Remain full of the Word at all times, so you will have the spiritual strength, wisdom, and discernment to hear and follow the voice of the Lord. Doing this will also counter (oppose; hinder) the enemy's attacks against you. When you neglect personal time spent in God's Word, you starve your spirit and lower your defenses against negative things that may try to sidetrack you; like depression, negative emotional reactions, offense, and frustration.

The Bible says the joy of the Lord is your strength. *Meditate* on the Word of God to maintain your confidence-connection with the Father. Reading the Bible is one thing, but when you take time to ponder and intensely think about each scripture and how it applies to your life, you get even more spiritual strength, understanding, and confidence from it.

Prayer is communication with God. Effective prayer is a combination of listening to God, praising God, and praying the Word of God by speaking it out loud, echoing to God what He has already declared. Praying the Word of God is also effective because of the power contained in the Scriptures.

STUDY QUESTIONS

1. What does a leader need to keep him operating in *confidence overflow*?

_____

_____

2. What can remaining full of the Word of God at all times do for a leader?

_____

_____

3. What does *Nehemiah 8:10 (NIV)* tell us about the joy of the Lord?

_____

_____

4. What happens when you take time to ponder and intensely think about each scripture and how it applies to your life?

_____

_____

_____

_____

5. What is prayer?

_____

_____

DISCUSSION QUESTIONS

1. What does it mean to *Meditate* on the Word of God?

   _____

   _____

   _____

2. What happens when you are sure that God has ordained you to start a ministry, open a business, or to make some type of big investment?

   _____

   _____

   _____

3. What does *'Effective Prayer'* consist of?

   _____

   _____

4. Why is *'Praying the Word of God'* so effective?

   _____

   _____

5. What does *Isaiah 55:11(NKJV)* mean when it says, "*So shall My Word be that goes forth from My mouth; It shall not return to Me void, But it shall accomplish what I please, And it shall prosper in the thing for which I sent it.*"

   _____

   _____

   _____

LIFE APPLICATION

On the following page, reflect and write about a time in your own life when you used *'God's Word + Prayer'* to increase your confidence as a leader.

*"When the leader lacks confidence,
the followers lack commitment."*

- John Maxwell

God's Word + Prayer = Leadership Confidence

Write & Reflect

_____

_____

_____

_____

_____

_____

_____

_____

_____

_____

_____

_____

_____

SCRIPTURES

Nehemiah said, "Go and enjoy choice food and sweet drinks, and send some to those who have nothing prepared. This day is holy to our Lord. Do not grieve, for the joy of the Lord is your strength."

Nehemiah 8:10 (NIV)

So shall My word be that goes forth from My mouth; It shall not return to Me void, But it shall accomplish what I please, And it shall prosper in the thing for which I sent it.

Isaiah 55:11 (NKJV)

"While the earth remains, Seedtime and harvest, Cold and heat, Winter and summer, And day and night Shall not cease."

Genesis 8:22 (NKJV)

Do not be deceived: God is not mocked, for whatever one sow, that will he also reap.

Galatians 6:7 (ESV)

INSPIRATIONAL QUOTES

"When the leader lacks confidence, the followers lack commitment."

__John Maxwell

LESSON 5

DEVELOPING YOUR LEADERSHIP CONFIDENCE
LESSON SUMMARY

Those whom God uses are not always the most talented, but those who have the best attitude and allow God to prepare them. But if we want God to use us, it will require obedience. If we want God to use us, we must work with Him to develop our leadership skills. Before God uses anyone, He prepares and equips them.

A confident leader is not necessarily someone who has a large organization or is in a position that influences thousands of people. A confident leader is someone who is on top of things in his or her realm of influence.

If you want to operate in your full leadership potential, start where you are, regardless if you feel everything is perfect or not. Do something now. Nobody starts at the finish line. Don't despise the day of small beginnings *(Zechariah 4:10)*.

STUDY QUESTIONS

1. The people God use are not always the most talented, but what do they have and what do they do?

   _____

   _____

2. What will it require if we want God to use us?

   _____

   _____

3. If we want God to use us, what must we work with Him to develop in our lives?

   _____

   _____

4. What does God do before He uses anyone?

   _____

   _____

5. True or False: A confident leader is someone who has a large organization and is in a position that influences thousands of people.

   _____

   _____

DISCUSSION QUESTIONS

1. What do you think the following statement mean? *"A confident leader is someone who is on top of things in his or her realm of influence."*

   _____

   _____

2. What should you do if you want to operate in your full leadership potential?

   _____

   _____

3. What does the phrase, *"Nobody starts at the finish line."* mean to you as a leader?

   _____

   _____

   _____

4. Read *Zechariah 4:10 (NLT)*. Explain this verse.

   _____

   _____

   _____

5. Write down one example of a small beginning.

   _____

   _____

LIFE APPLICATION

On the following page, think and write about the action steps you plan to take to develop your leadership confidence.

"The trust of the people in the leaders reflects the confidence of the leaders in the people."

- Paulo Freire

Developing Your Leadership Confidence

Write & Reflect

_____

_____

_____

_____

_____

_____

_____

_____

_____

_____

_____

_____

SCRIPTURE

Do not despise these small beginnings, for the Lord rejoices to see the work begin, to see the plumb line in Zerubbabel's hand.

Zechariah 4:10 (NLT)

INSPIRATIONAL QUOTE

"The trust of the people in the leaders reflects the confidence of the leaders in the people."

__Paulo Freire

LESSON 6

FOLLOW THE LEADER

LESSON SUMMARY

Have you ever played the game, *Follow the Leader? Follow the Leader is* a familiar game that is played and enjoyed by children all over the world. In our own lives as adults, we also play *Follow the Leader.* We follow leaders at church, at school, in sports, in our government, and in other areas of our lives. We have to make sure we choose a leader who will lead us in the right direction. We have a Leader who we can depend on to always lead us in the right direction. The Leader who is guaranteed to lead us right without fail is the Holy Spirit.

God knows what is best for our lives. God is God, and He sees the big picture. We *think* we know. That is why we need to be led by the Holy Spirit, especially if we are leaders. The Word of God says that the Spirit of truth will guide us into all truth.

Whatever the Holy Spirit leads you to do always lines up with the written Word of God. As you renew your mind with the Word of God and recognize the voice of the Holy Spirit in your life, the Holy Spirit will lead you into a life of abundance, peace, joy, protection, and success. To recognize the voice of the Holy Spirit, we must spend time in the Word of God and prayer.

As leaders, in order to be a great leader, we have to follow the Leader of Leaders, God. God is our Role Model. The Leader of all leaders is God: The Ultimate Leader. God gives us the power to lead. That power is the power of the Holy Spirit. Start following the Leader, the Holy Spirit, today, and watch your confidence to lead others soar!

STUDY QUESTIONS

1. Read *Proverbs 16:9 (TLB)*. According to this verse, we should make plans, but what else should we do?

   _____

   _____

2. Read *Proverbs 21:2 (TLB)*. How does this verse relate to a person's motives?

   _____

   _____

   _____

3. Read *John 16:13 (MEV)*. According to this verse, what will the Holy Spirit guide us into?

   _____

   _____

4. Whatever the Holy Spirit leads you to do, always lines up with what?

   _____

   _____

5. What do we have to do in order to recognize the voice of the Holy Spirit?

   _____

   _____

DISCUSSION QUESTIONS

1. Who is a Leader we can depend on to always lead us in the right direction and is guaranteed to lead us right without fail? Why?

_____

_____

_____

2. How do we *renew our minds*?

_____

_____

3. Why do you think it is so important for a leader to be led by the Holy Spirit?

_____

_____

_____

4. Read *Proverbs 3:5-6 (AMPC).* Can you think of an example of how you have applied these verses to your own life and the Lord has directed and made your path straight and plain?

_____

_____

5. The Bible tells us in *John 14:16 (AMPC)* that the Holy Spirit is our Comforter. According to this verse, what are six other words for Comforter?

_____

_____

LIFE APPLICATION

On the following page, reflect and write about a time in your life when you followed the Leader, the Holy Spirit.

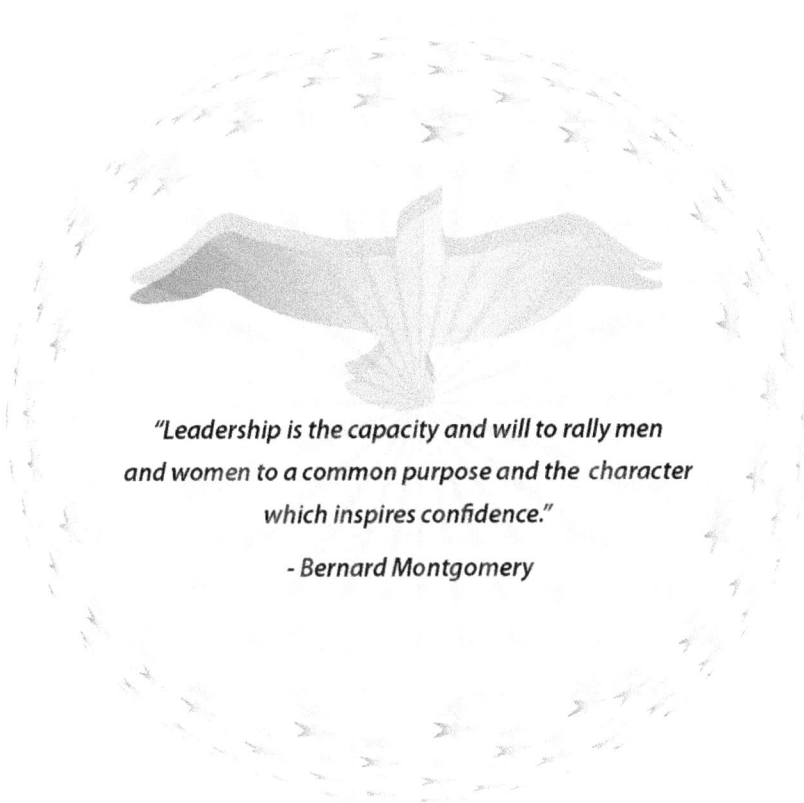

"Leadership is the capacity and will to rally men and women to a common purpose and the character which inspires confidence."

- Bernard Montgomery

Follow The Leader

Write & Reflect

_____

_____

_____

_____

_____

_____

_____

_____

_____

_____

_____

_____

_____

SCRIPTURES

A man's heart plans his way, But the Lord directs his steps.

__ Proverbs 16:9 (NKJV)

We should make plans --counting on God to direct us.

__ Proverbs 16:9 (TLB)

We can justify our every deed, but God looks at our motives.

Proverbs 21:2(TLB)

But when the Spirit of truth comes, He will guide you into all truth. For He will not speak on His own authority. But He will speak whatever He hears, and He will tell you things that are to come.

__John 16:13 (MEV)

Lean on, trust in, and be confident in the Lord with all your heart and mind and do not rely on your own insight or understanding. In all your ways know, recognize, and acknowledge Him, and He will direct and make straight and plain your paths.

Proverbs 3:5-6 (AMPC)

And I will ask the Father, and He will give you another Comforter (Counselor, Helper, Intercessor, Advocate, Strengthener, and Standby), that He may remain with you forever.

John14:16 (AMPC)

Now may the God of peace Himself sanctify you completely; and may your whole spirit, soul, and body be preserved blameless at the coming of our Lord Jesus Christ.

1 Thessalonians 5:23 (NKJV)

INSPIRATIONAL QUOTE

"Leadership is the capacity and will to rally men and women to a common purpose and the character which inspires confidence."

__Bernard Montgomery

LESSON 7

GROWING AS A CONFIDENT LEADER

LESSON SUMMARY

An organization can only go as far as the leadership. If you are not growing or making progress, your organization will become stagnant. Leaders who aren't maturing will oversee others who aren't moving to the next level.

Growth and maturity are essential. Other people suffer when you, the leader, has not dealt with emotional problems, or if your spiritual life is not on point. When you lack confidence or feel out of control in your own life, most likely, you will attempt to control other people. This leads to stressful relationships with others. It then becomes vital that you deal with these issues through God's Word so you can move to your next level.

Effective leadership involves relational skills. Be direct and honest, but make sure your heart is in the right place. You can be the confident leader God has called you to be by developing in the areas of relational skills. By using God's Word as your guide and allowing the Holy Spirit to teach you how to interact with others, you will develop loyal followers who can carry out your vision in excellence.

A confident leader must first and foremost be a servant. A servant is willing to do whatever is necessary to be a blessing to others. It is the leader who goes above and beyond what is asked of him, not because he or she *has* to, but because they *want* to. This leader is not concerned with being recognized. Instead, it is simply to please God. The love of God makes a leader want to serve others. The leader who has a servant's heart has released selfishness and is consumed with meeting the needs of people, even if he or she has to be inconvenienced.

STUDY QUESTIONS

1. An organization can only go as far as the _____.

2. What happens when a leader has not dealt with his emotional problems or spiritual life?

   _____

   _____

3. What does effective leadership involve?

   _____

   _____

4. It is ok for a leader to be direct and honest, but he must make sure what is in the right place?

   _____

   _____

5. A confident leader must first, and foremost, be a _____.

DISCUSSION QUESTIONS

1. What are the ingredients of true leadership?

   _____

   _____

2. When a leader lacks confidence or feels out of control in his or her own life, how does this affect other people?

   _____

   _____

3. How can a leader develop loyal followers??

   _____

   _____

   _____

4. What does it mean for a leader to have a servant's heart?

   _____

   _____

   _____

5. What do you think make a leader want to serve others?

   _____

   _____

LIFE APPLICATION

Explain why growth and maturity are so essential for a leader. What can happen to a leader, his organization, or those whom he or she leads when the leader stops growing? Use the chart on the following page to write your answer.

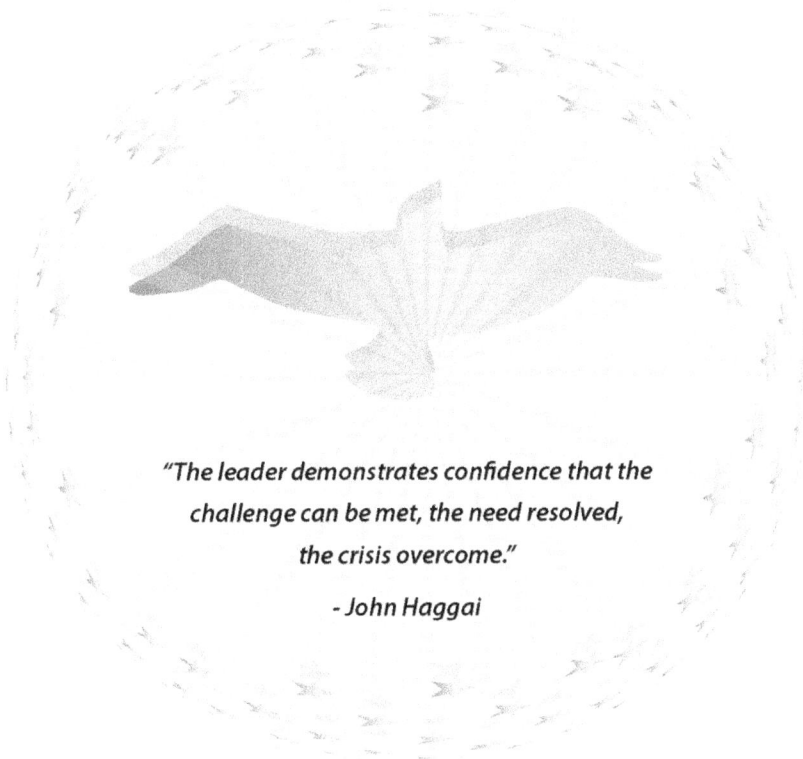

"The leader demonstrates confidence that the challenge can be met, the need resolved, the crisis overcome."

- John Haggai

Leadership Growth And Development

Write & Reflect

_____

_____

_____

_____

_____

_____

_____

_____

_____

_____

_____

_____

_____

_____

SCRIPTURES

But he that is greatest among you shall be your servant.

Matthew 23:11 (KJV)

And he sat down, and called the twelve, and saith unto them, If any man desire to be first, the same shall be last of all, and servant of all.

Mark 9:35 (KJV)

INSPIRATIONAL QUOTES

"The leader demonstrates confidence that the challenge can be met, the need resolved, the crisis overcome."

__John Haggai

LESSON 8

LEADING WITH CONFIDENCE

LESSON SUMMARY

Confidence is a key to success in leadership. Confidence is also the foundation of leadership. The leader must have this strong foundation to be able to transfer it to his or her followers. It is only with confidence that you, as a leader, will be able to provide a foundation for your followers.

You are that solid rock upon which your followers depend on to be the example they need to grow and develop as leaders. Followers need to see the stability in their leader, and they are looking for you to produce the stability that they might not have themselves. Confidence is an essential quality of leadership on which all the other qualities of leadership depends or is based.

If the leader does not have confidence in him or herself, effective leadership will not exist. A leader who is highly qualified and have many skills, but lacks confidence, will have a difficult time leading others.

Leadership confidence is a more crucial asset than knowledge, skill, or experience. Without confidence, a leader will find it hard to make difficult decisions, lead with authority, communicate effectively with others, or to take smart risks. Confidence is what separates average leaders from great leaders.

STUDY QUESTIONS

1. How can you, as a leader, provide a foundation for your followers?

_____

_____

2. What can happen when a leader is highly qualified and has many skills, but lacks confidence?

_____

_____

_____

_____

3. True or False: Leadership confidence is a more crucial asset than knowledge, skill, or experience.

_____

4. Without confidence, a leader will find it hard to make difficult _____ , lead with _____ , _____ effectively with others, or to take smart _____.

5. What separates average leaders from great leaders?

_____

_____

DISCUSSION QUESTIONS

1. How can a leader improve his or her confidence?

_____

_____

_____

2. How can a leader build confidence in others?

_____

_____

_____

3. How is becoming an excellent leader a process?

_____

_____

4. How can you, a leader, be that *solid rock* upon which your followers can depend on to be the example they need to grow and develop as leaders?

_____

_____

_____

5. Followers need to see the stability in their leaders that they might not have themselves. Give three examples of this stability in a leader.

_____

_____

_____

LIFE APPLICATION

Using the chart on the following page, write about a confident leader who was a role model, and made a positive impact on your life.

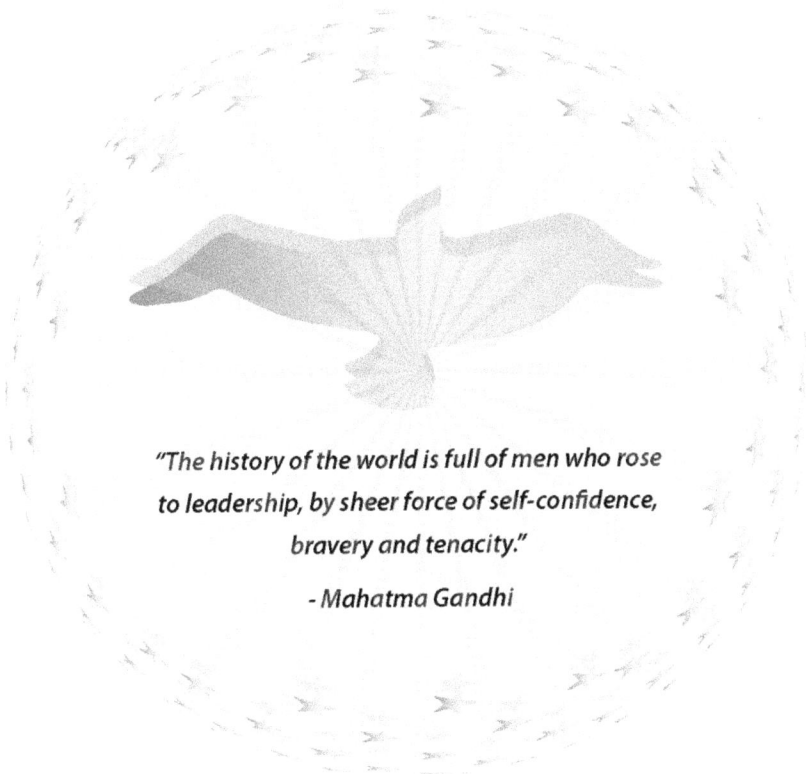

"The history of the world is full of men who rose to leadership, by sheer force of self-confidence, bravery and tenacity."

- Mahatma Gandhi

My Role Model

Write & Reflect

_____

_____

_____

_____

_____

_____

_____

_____

_____

_____

_____

_____

_____

SCRIPTURES

And this is the confidence that we have toward him, that if we ask anything according to his will he hears us.

1 John 5:14 (ESV)

So we say with confidence, "The Lord is my helper; I will not be afraid. What can mere mortals do to me?"

Hebrews 13:6 (NIV)

INSPIRATIONAL QUOTES

"The history of the world is full of men who rose to leadership, by sheer force of self-confidence, bravery and tenacity."

__Mahatma Gandhi

"Self-confidence is the fundamental basis from which leadership grows. Trying to teach leadership without first building confidence is like building a house on a foundation of sand. It may have a nice coat of paint, but it is ultimately shaky at best."

__Francisco Dao

NOTES

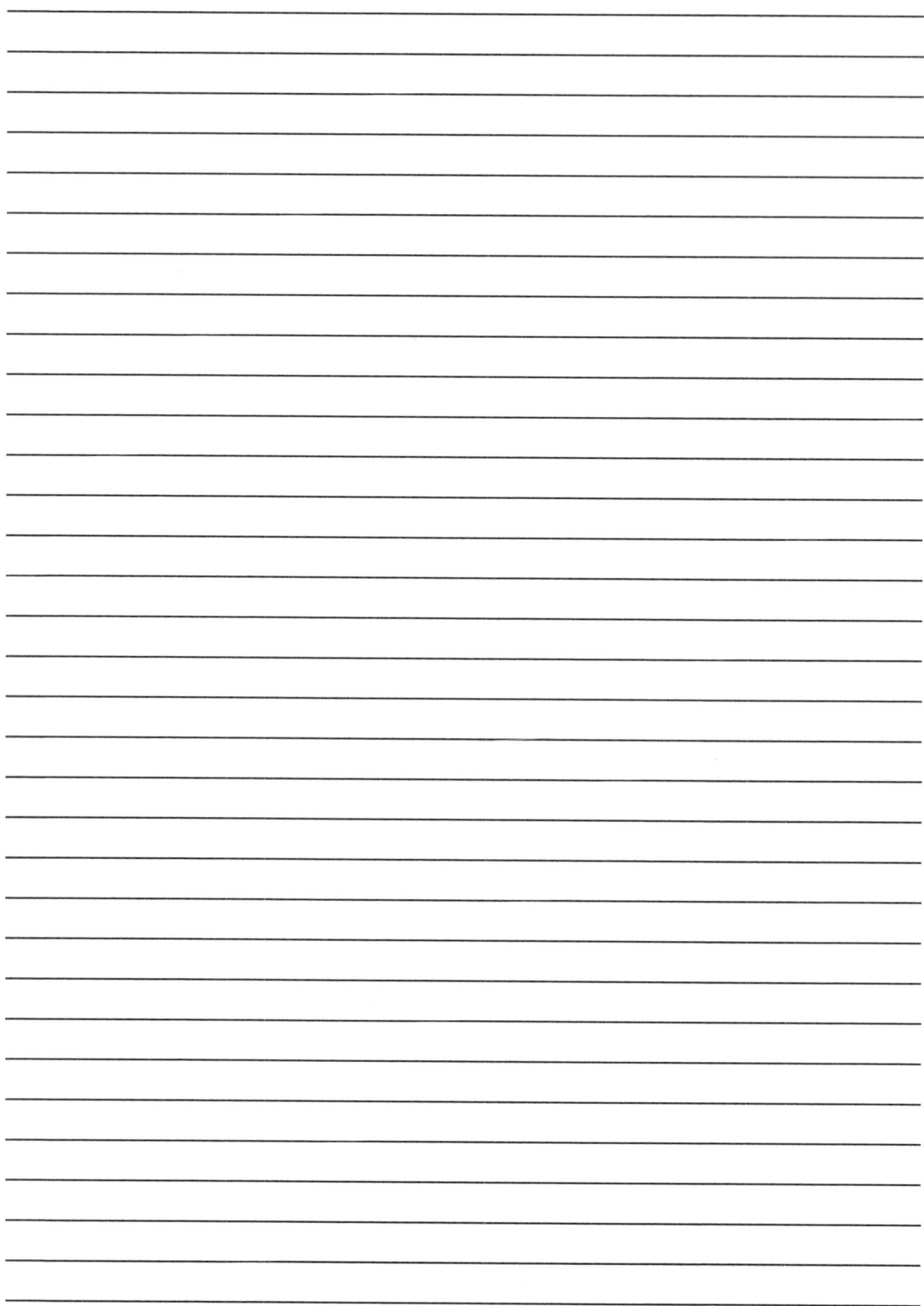

PRAYER FOR A RELATIONSHIP WITH JESUS

If you have never accepted Jesus as your personal Savior, you can do so right now.

If you would like to receive Christ by faith, pray this simple prayer:

Dear Lord, I acknowledge that I am a sinner. I believe Jesus died for my sins and rose again.

I repent of my sins. By faith, I receive the Lord Jesus Christ as my Savior.

I believe right now that the Lord Jesus is my personal Savior, and that all my sins are forgiven through His precious blood.

I thank You, dear Lord, for saving me.

In Jesus' name, Amen.

If you prayed this prayer, God heard you and saved you. I personally want to welcome you to the family of God!

ANSWERS

ANSWER KEY

LESSON 1
CHARACTERISTICS OF A CONFIDENT LEADER

1. Remain calm under pressure, give people clear directives, and inspire others
2. Being forceful and direct
3. Trust or faith, a feeling of assurance, especially self-assurance, security
4. The writer of *Hebrews* urges us not to throw away our confidence because it will be richly rewarded.
5. Influence, faithfulness, and ability

LESSON 2
A CONFIDENT LEADER GETS RESULTS

1. A leader's true leadership ability is shown how smoothly the organization runs when the leader is not around.
2. The lack of proper orientation and training
3. To *orient* means to make someone familiar with something or to acquaint with the existing situation or environment *(Webster)*
4. The training begins
5. Yourself, decisions

LESSON 3
CONFIDENT LEADERS REPRODUCE CONFIDENT LEADERS

1. The leader must first demonstrate those qualities in his own life.
2. Character and Integrity
3. It creates a standard others will want to follow.
4. Good leaders abhor (despise, hate) wrongdoing of all kinds. Sound leadership has a moral foundation.
5. Maintaining contact with your Heavenly Father daily

LESSON 4
GOD'S WORD + PRAYER = CONFIDENCE

1. The Word of God which is spiritual food
2. The leader will have the spiritual strength, wisdom, and discernment to hear and follow the voice of the Lord. Doing this will also counter (oppose, hinder) the enemy's attacks against the leader.

3. The joy of the Lord is your strength.
4. You get even more spiritual strength, understanding, and confidence from it.
5. Prayer is communication with God.

LESSON 5
DEVELOPING YOUR LEADERSHIP CONFIDENCE

1. They have the best attitude, and they allow God to prepare them.
2. It will require obedience.
3. We must work with God to develop our leadership skills.
4. He prepares and equips them.
5. False

LESSON 6
FOLLOW THE LEADER

1. We should count on (rely on, depend on, trust) God to direct us.
2. God looks at our motives.
3. All Truth
4. The written Word of God
5. We must spend time in the Word of God and prayer.

LESSON 7
GROWING AS A CONFIDENT LEADER

1. Leadership
2. The people he leads will suffer.
3. Relational skills
4. His heart
5. Servant

LESSON 8
LEADING WITH CONFIDENCE

1. With confidence
2. The leader will have a difficult time leading others.
3. True
4. Decisions, authority, communicate, risks
5. Confidence

ABOUT THE AUTHOR

MIRANDA BURNETTE is the president and founder of Miranda Burnette Ministries, Inc. She is a licensed evangelist. She is also the founder of Keys to Success Academy, Inc., an Online Leadership Bible School. Miranda teaches people how to discover and fulfill their calling, to make their dreams a reality, to be successful in every area of their lives, and to be all God created them to be. The vision of Miranda Burnette Ministries is to educate, equip, and empower others to be successful leaders and reach their full God-given potential.

Miranda is the author of *Success Starts in Your Mind, Dare to Dream and Soar like an Eagle, Leader to Leader, Keys to Living a Fruit-Filled Life, Dare to Dream Again – Book and Study Guide,* and *Winning With the Power of Love – Book and Study Guide.* She also makes an impact on the lives of others with her teachings on CD. She is the founder and president of I Can Christian Academy, Inc. Miranda and her husband, Morris, lives in Atlanta, Georgia, and are the parents of two adult children, LaTrelle and Davin.

CONTACT INFORMATION

For more information or to order books contact:

Miranda Burnette Ministries, Inc.
P. O. Box 314
Clarkdale, GA 30111

E-mail:
Miranda@ mirandaburnetteministries.org

Website:
www.mirandaburnetteministries.org

OTHER BOOKS BY MIRANDA BURNETTE

Dare to Dream and Soar Like an Eagle
The Sky is the Limit!

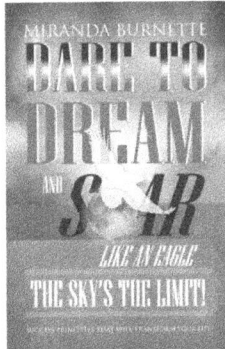

    If you are ready to take the challenge to make your dreams a reality, this book is for you. In these pages, Miranda Burnette shares important success principles that will absolutely transform your life. The keys contained in this powerful book will help you soar from level to level to fulfill God's purpose for your life.

Dare to Dream and Soar like an Eagle will help you:

- Maximize your potential
- Achieve your goals
- Clarify your vision
- Cultivate inspired ideas
- Release the seeds of greatness that God has placed inside you.
- Recognize that God created you for *SUCCESS*

    It doesn't matter who you are or what you are experiencing in your life right now, you have residing within you God-given ability to accomplish more than you could ever imagine. So *Dare to Dream and Soar Like an Eagle! The Sky's the Limit!*

Success Starts In Your Mind
A Manual on How to Think Your Way to Success

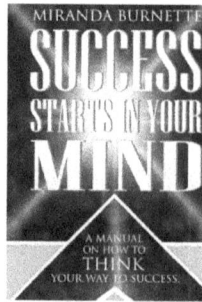

If you could change one thing in your life right now, what would you change? Have you ever considered changing your thoughts? If you are frustrated, discontented, and disappointed with your life, if you want to be successful in different areas of your life, if you want to be freed from the bondage of bad habits, and if you want your life to change, *THIS BOOK IS FOR YOU!*

If you want your life to change, you have to change your thinking. Your life won't change unless your thoughts change. You can change your life by changing your thoughts.

SUCCESS STARTS IN YOUR MIND will help you:
- Understand the power of thoughts
- Develop an understanding of the relationship between success and the mind
- Think positively
- Overcome the fear of success
- Comprehend how what you think about yourself can dramatically affect your level of success
- Realize that *Success Starts In Your Mind*

If you are not successful, or if you are not as successful as you would like to be, it is time for you to start *Thinking Your Way to Success.*

Leader to Leader
Inspiring Words for Women in Leadership

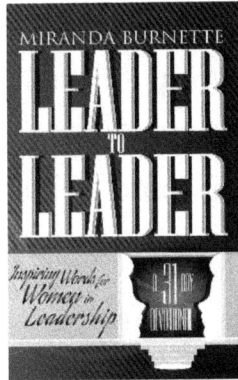

Do you want to be a strong, confident leader? Do you want to learn leadership principles that will take you and your organization to the next level? Do you desire to develop leaders, not just followers? Do you want to learn how to make good decisions? *THEN THIS BOOK IS FOR YOU!*

LEADER TO LEADER will help you to:

- Discover how to be an effective leader
- Develop principles of leadership that will help you be the leader others will follow
- Learn the qualities of a great leader
- Realize that failure is not fatal
- Use your past mistakes as a stepping stone to rise to the next level
- Lead by example
- Develop great leaders

Read, study, and meditate on the leadership principles in this devotional and become the effective leader you've always wanted to be!

Keys to Living a Fruit-Filled Life
Nine Keys That Will Unlock the Door to Success in Your Life

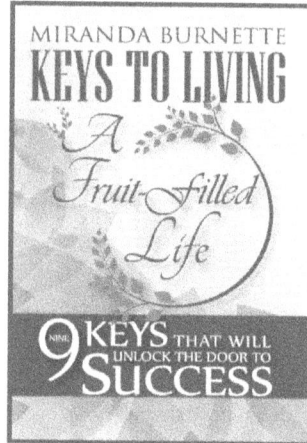

Do you want to have a successful, productive, fulfilling life? Would you like to have a life where you accomplish great things? Have you been desiring a life where you are constantly growing and overflowing with blessings and prosperity? Do you want a life that is producing good fruit? Would you like to live your life in such a way that you make a great difference in the lives of others? Do you want a life that is full of love, joy, peace, patience, kindness, goodness, humility, faithfulness, and self-control? If you answered yes to all of those questions, *THIS BOOK IS FOR YOU!*

Keys to Living a Fruit-Filled Life will teach you:

- How to live a happier more peaceful life
- How to prepare for great opportunities
- Steps to develop the Fruit of the Spirit in your life
- How to develop great relationships
- Nine keys that will unlock the door to success in your life
- How to live the *"Good Life"*

Keys to Living a Fruit-Filled Life will open the door to success in your life and guide you into how to enjoy the abundant life God has for you.

Dare to Dream Again!
It's Never Too Late for a New Beginning
Book and Study

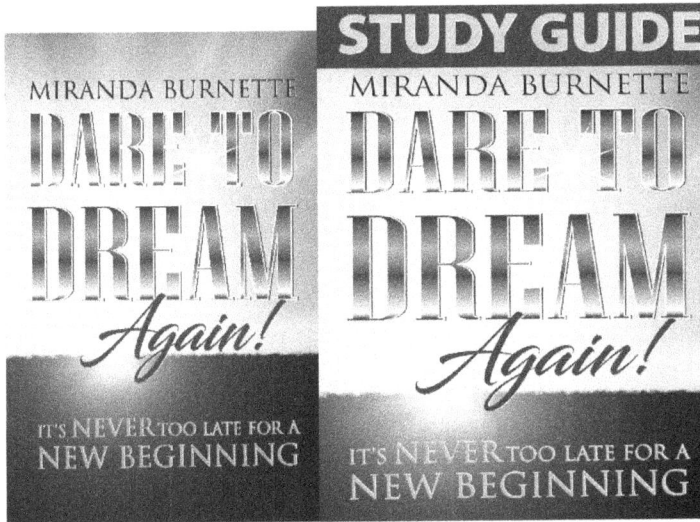

Have you ever dreamed of winning something, being something, or starting something? Maybe you have dreamed of starting your own business, earning a degree, becoming a professional athlete, artist, or musician.

We are born dreamers! When you stop dreaming, it seems as if a part of you is missing. Nothing else seems to fulfill you as much as the desire to realize or accomplish your dream.

God has a specific plan designed for each of our lives. Nevertheless, it is our responsibility to stay on the path to our dream. We must hold on to the dream, cooperate with God, and fulfill the plan He has for our lives. If you have lost sight of your dream, and given up on your dream, it is time to dream again!

As you read this book, it is my sincere prayer that you will pick up the shattered pieces of your dream and rekindle the passion you once had and *Dare to Dream Again!* Once you start dreaming again, this time, don't let anyone or anything stop you from living your dream! Hold on to your dream and don't let it go!

Winning With the Power of Love
How to Love Your Way to Victory
Book and Study Guide

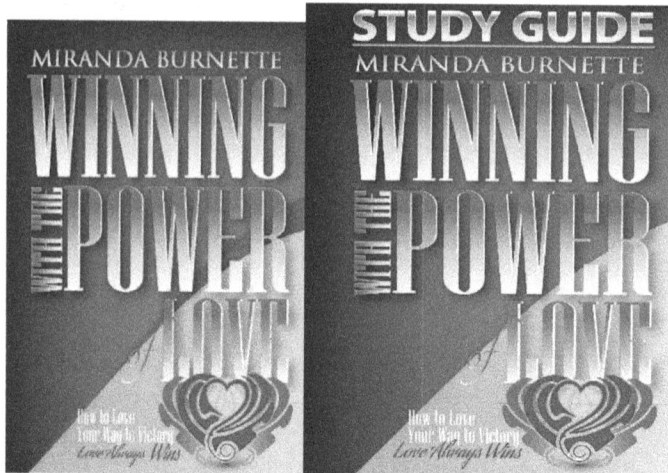

Do you want to be a winner in life? Do you want to reach your goals, be successful, have good relationships, and prosper in every area of your life? Do you want to have joy, peace, and happiness abounding in your life? Do you want to make a difference in the lives of others and help them to succeed and be winners? If your answer to all of these questions is *YES,* this book is for you!

Winning with the Power of Love will help you to be the winner you have always dreamed you could be. This book contains the tools you need to overcome obstacles that have been holding you back and reach your full God-given potential.

Winning with the Power of Love will teach you:

- The true meaning of being a winner
- How the power of love can literally change your life
- How to win with people
- How to win by loving yourself
- Why love is so powerful
- How the force of love will drive fear out of your life forever
- How walking in the power of love can increase your faith
- How many of your problems can be solved by you receiving God's love, loving yourself, loving God and loving others

If you are not loving, you are not winning. You can't lose when you love. Love has never lost a battle, and it never will. You can win with the power of love. Start loving and start winning today. Building your life on the solid foundation of love will enable you to accomplish more in life than you could ever imagine.

www.ingramcontent.com/pod-product-compliance
Lightning Source LLC
Chambersburg PA
CBHW081515040426
42447CB00013B/3235